COPYRIGHT © 2022 GOODHEARTED BOOKS INC.

info@goodheartedbooks.com

ISBN: 978-1-988779-60-7

Dépôt légal : bibliothèque et archives nationales du Québec, 2022.
Dépôt légal : bibliothèque et archives Canada, 2022.

Created by	: Bachar Karroum
Graphic Designer	: Samuel Gabriel
Cover Designer	: Creative Hands
Content revision	: Omar Ahmad, Safa Said, Mohamed Ali
Proofreader	: Christine Campbell

IN THE NAME OF ALLAH

Bringing this practical book to life for you and your little ones has been an inspiring journey. We are grateful to be able to build on our series of books to share the essence of Islam with children. This creation has been specially crafted to shine a light on the most important personality traits of Prophet Mohammad (PBUH), the noblest man of all time.

We hope that you and your family members will enjoy this learning experience and that it will help your children become the best version of themselves while spreading the beautiful values of our beloved religion.

GLOSSARY

Abu Bakr (RA)	: The first caliph of Islam
Allah	: The Arabic word for God
Akhira	: Afterlife
Dunya	: Life on earth
Hudaibiya	: A city near Makkah in actual Saudi Arabia
Jannah	: Paradise
Kaaba	: The cubic structure at al-Haram Mosque in Makkah
Makkah	: The spiritual center of Islam
Madinah	: The second-holiest city in Islam
PBUH	: Peace be upon him
Quraish	: Arab people before Islam
RA (Radiallahu anhum)	: May Allah be pleased with them
Siwak	: A natural toothbrush prepared from the branches of various trees
Ta'if	: A city in the Makkan Region of Saudi Arabia
Umar (RA)	: The second caliph of Islam
Wudhu	: Ablution

ACCOUNTABLE

Being accountable means taking responsibility for your actions and being expected to justify them when asked.

EXPERIENCE LIVED BY PROPHET MOHAMMAD (PBUH)

Prophet Mohammad (PBUH) had a great sense of accountability. He held himself accountable for spreading the message of Islam in the best manner possible. In his last sermon, he prayed "O Allah! Be Witness (I have conveyed Your Message)."[1] He also felt deeply about worldly affairs and how

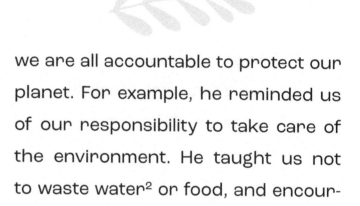

we are all accountable to protect our planet. For example, he reminded us of our responsibility to take care of the environment. He taught us not to waste water[2] or food, and encouraged us to keep our land clean and plant more trees.[3]

POSITIVE LESSON I CAN LEARN FROM OUR PROPHET (PBUH)

When you're personally accountable for a role, it means that you take ownership of your choices or actions. For example, you are accountable for doing your homework, or cleaning your room every morning; therefore, you are responsible to complete your tasks. Being accountable means that you do not make excuses if you don't fulfill your work. We should always do our best to accomplish our responsibilities. This will teach us to honor our commitment just like our Prophet (PBUH) did.

2
BRAVE

Being brave means not showing fear when facing danger or difficulties.

Prophet Mohammad (PBUH) feared none but Allah. When he started teaching people about Islam, Quraish threatened and tried to hurt him. But he was brave enough to continue his mission of spreading Islam. Once, he was sleeping under a tree; when he woke up, he found a man holding his unsheathed sword and asked, "Who will save you from me?" Prophet Mohammad (PBUH) wasn't scared and said "Allah" three times in complete confidence. Prophet Mohammad (PBUH) did not punish him but sat down with him.[4]

POSITIVE LESSON I CAN LEARN FROM OUR PROPHET (PBUH)

Bravery is an essential trait that is taught in Islam. Being brave allows you to face difficulties and your fears, like asking questions in class or speaking in front of many people. Standing up and allowing yourself to feel difficult emotions, and not letting them defeat you, is a sign of bravery. Doing so strengthens your personality and helps you improve at school and everyday life. Go ahead, do the things that scare you, as it will allow you to move forward and be strong in any situation.

3

CALM

Calm means being peaceful, quiet, and without worry.

EXPERIENCE LIVED BY PROPHET MOHAMMAD (PBUH)

Prophet Mohammad (PBUH) had a really calm personality. He would not get angry quickly. Once, a man came to him and pulled his garment harshly and asked for something to be given from what Allah had given him. Prophet Mohammad (PBUH) smiled and instructed his companions to give

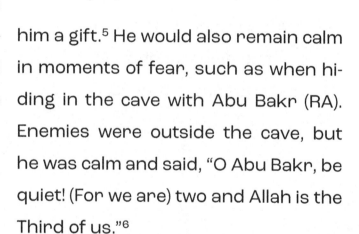

him a gift.[5] He would also remain calm in moments of fear, such as when hiding in the cave with Abu Bakr (RA). Enemies were outside the cave, but he was calm and said, "O Abu Bakr, be quiet! (For we are) two and Allah is the Third of us."[6]

POSITIVE LESSON I CAN LEARN FROM OUR PROPHET (PBUH)

Like Prophet Mohammad (PBUH), you can try to always remain calm when facing a difficult or challenging situation. If your sibling or friend bothers you, staying calm and avoiding anger will help avoid a fight and strengthen your patience and personality.

Remaining calm in a tough situation will also encourage others to listen to you and pay attention to your point of view. Calmness fosters empathy and helps create a better and more peaceful world.

4

CARING

A caring person is kind and gives emotional support to others.

Prophet Mohammad (PBUH) deeply cared for all his companions. He would inquire about someone if he didn't see him for three days. Once, a child was crying while he was leading the prayers. He shortened his prayer so the child's mother would not become distressed because of the crying.[7] Out of his care for others, he ordered his companions to make things easier for others.[8] He even cared about the feelings of his captives and demanded that they stay together with their families.[9]

POSITIVE LESSON I CAN LEARN FROM OUR PROPHET (PBUH)

Caring for others starts at home. For example, providing support to your parents by helping them with different tasks at home shows that you care about them. Being available to your friends when they are sad or listening to your sibling share a happy moment after school means that you are a caring person. When we care for others, just like our Prophet (PBUH), we contribute to spreading love and mercy in our society.

5

EQUAL

Being equal means treating people equally, regardless of race, social status, or conditions.

EXPERIENCE LIVED BY PROPHET MOHAMMAD (PBUH)

In the beginning, most of the followers of Prophet Mohammad (PBUH) were weak and poor. The rich said they would follow him if he left these vulnerable people, but he (PBUH) refused to leave the weak. He firmly believed that all people are made equal. In his last sermon, he said that no white man is better than black, and no Arab is better than non-Arab, but only those who are better Muslims.[10] He proved to all equality when he appointed a formerly enslaved Black person named Bilal as the prayer caller.[11]

POSITIVE LESSON I CAN LEARN FROM OUR PROPHET (PBUH)

Just like Prophet Mohammad (PBUH), you should treat everyone the same. If you meet a friend at school who is different from you, you should treat him or her like everyone else. Whether your classmates are sick, disabled, come from a different background, race, religion, or culture, you should treat them all with kindness and respect. Everyone, every human, deserves to be treated equally. Being equal with all will help improve justice in society.

6

FORGIVING

A forgiving person is a person willing to forgive. He pardons others for their actions or errors.

EXPERIENCE LIVED BY PROPHET MOHAMMAD (PBUH)

While preaching Islam, Prophet Mohammad (PBUH) was abused by non-believers in many ways. They hurt him and his followers. But he never held grudges against anyone. When he conquered Makkah, the disbelievers were scared that now Prophet Mohammad (PBUH) had all the power to take revenge. But he forgave everyone and allowed everyone to stay in Makkah in peace and security.[12] He also advised his followers to forgive others so Allah may forgive them in return.

POSITIVE LESSON I CAN LEARN FROM OUR PROPHET (PBUH)

Being forgiving is one of the best traits you can learn from the Prophet Mohammad (PBUH). If your siblings or friends hurt your feelings, try to speak and listen to them to understand the reasons behind their actions or behaviors. This will make it easier to forgive. When you forgive someone, you remove all negative emotions form your heart. Allah loves those who forgive.

7

GENEROUS

Being generous means being willing to give money, help, show kindness, etc., more than it is expected.

EXPERIENCE LIVED BY PROPHET MOHAMMAD (PBUH)

Prophet Mohammad (PBUH) would never say no to anyone who asked him for something, even if he had nothing left for himself. Once, he received a cloak from a woman. A man liked it and asked him (PBUH) to give it to him. He gave away the cloak even though he needed it.[13]

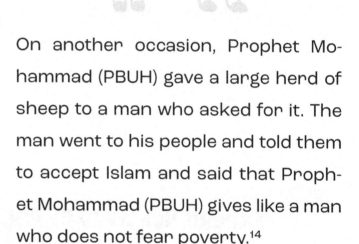

On another occasion, Prophet Mohammad (PBUH) gave a large herd of sheep to a man who asked for it. The man went to his people and told them to accept Islam and said that Prophet Mohammad (PBUH) gives like a man who does not fear poverty.[14]

POSITIVE LESSON I CAN LEARN FROM OUR PROPHET (PBUH)

You can be generous like our Prophet Mohammad (PBUH) by giving some of your favorite toys or clothes to those in need. You can also be generous with your time by helping a sibling or a friend with something he needs to do or to understand. Being generous will increase our faith and love in Allah. It helps spread goodness in our world.

8

GOD-FEARING

God-fearing is someone who submits to Allah and follows His guidance.

Prophet Mohammad (PBUH) said he was the most God-fearing among people.[15] Allah had already pardoned him and granted him the news of paradise. Still, he would ask Allah's forgiveness more than seventy times a day.[16] His every action was according to the commands of Allah. He used to cry from the fear that his disobedient people might go to hell, and Allah would be angry with them. This fear motivated him to continue his mission of spreading Allah's words to everyone.

POSITIVE LESSON I CAN LEARN FROM OUR PROPHET (PBUH)

Fearing Allah by submitting to Him and following His guidance, just like our Prophet (PBUH) did, helps us become better and stronger people. Being God-fearing means that we carry God in our thoughts daily, which helps us avoid bad deeds and encourages us to do good in this world by spreading love and peace. If you are facing a difficult situation at school, you can think of Him, remember His love and His words to help you make a good decision.

GREAT SPEAKER

A great speaker is a person who can give a speech that inspires.

EXPERIENCE LIVED BY PROPHET MOHAMMAD (PBUH)

Prophet Mohammad (PBUH) used to speak slowly and clearly so that everyone could understand each word. He would repeat essential things three times[17] to ensure no one missed them. His words captured hearts and souls. Even his enemies had to admit to this quality. He used appropriate hand gestures, smiles, and eye contact to connect with his audience.

He would engage them by questioning, probing, or joking. He would advise people in private and, for more significant issues, he would advise the whole gathering without directly mentioning anyone so that no one was embarrassed and everyone learned the lesson.

POSITIVE LESSON I CAN LEARN FROM OUR PROPHET (PBUH)

You can learn the art of public speaking from our Prophet (PBUH). One of the best ways to improve this is by practicing. The more you practice speaking in front of a group, the better you become. In addition, reading books can significantly improve your speaking. Practicing and reading will help you spread the good words around you.

GUARDIAN

A guardian is someone who protects someone or something.

EXPERIENCE LIVED BY PROPHET MOHAMMAD (PBUH)

Prophet Mohammad (PBUH) was known as al-Amin (the trustworthy) since he was a young boy. People used to give him their valuables to keep them safe. Prophet Mohammad (PBUH) guarded those valuables with all his heart. Even when the disbelievers wanted to harm him while he was migrating to Madinah, he didn't forget about the things he was protecting. Many of these belonged to his enemies, but instead of using them to threaten his enemies, he ordered 'Ali (RA) to stay behind and return everything to its rightful owner.[18]

I CAN BE A GUARDIAN TOO

POSITIVE LESSON I CAN LEARN FROM OUR PROPHET (PBUH)

Just like Prophet Mohammad (PBUH), you should be a sincere guardian and do your best to protect what you have been asked to keep safe. When a sibling or friend lets you borrow a toy or a book, you should do your best to keep it in good shape and avoid losing it. This show others that you can be trusted.

11

HAVE DIGNITY

To have dignity means being worthy of honor or respect.

EXPERIENCE LIVED BY PROPHET MOHAMMAD (PBUH)

Prophet Mohammad (PBUH) was a dignified man. He had firm principles, which he never compromised in any situation. He was a just and honest man who never lied or acted with prejudice, even during the war. He set clear rules for combat, like not harming the elderly, children, women,

livestock, infrastructure, trees, etc. When the people of Madinah secretly met him, they suggested attacking Meccans at night without warning. Prophet Mohammad (PBUH) refused and said it was not following his message.[19]

POSITIVE LESSON I CAN LEARN FROM OUR PROPHET (PBUH)

You can follow our prophet's steps by having dignity and carrying yourself well. This can be achieved by being poised or showing good values, like being honest and truthful. You can apply this by showing your parents or teacher respect. By having dignity, you are respecting yourself and, in turn, others respect you.

12

HELPFUL

Being helpful is to be willing to help, to be useful.

Prophet Mohammad (PBUH) was always willing to help others in whatever way he could. He would help with house chores and other duties. He would help the elderly by carrying their burdens. He would help to free enslaved people by providing financial support.

Once, during a journey, the companions divided the tasks involved in preparing food among themselves, like slaughtering, skinning, and cooking the sheep. Prophet Mohammad (PBUH) participated by collecting firewood because he wanted to help.[20]

ARE YOU OK,SISTER?

POSITIVE LESSON I CAN LEARN FROM OUR PROPHET (PBUH)

Like Prophet Mohammad (PBUH), we should always pay attention to those who need help. Never hesitate to lend a hand to a friend who is struggling with homework or if your parents need help with chores at home. Being helpful makes the job easier for everyone and encourages others to help you when needed.

13

HONEST

An honest person always tells the truth and can be trusted.

EXPERIENCE LIVED BY PROPHET MOHAMMAD (PBUH)

Prophet Mohammad (PBUH) was known for his honesty since his youth. Once, the tribes of Makkah argued about which tribe would get the honor of placing the black stone in its proper place in Kaaba. They agreed to let Mohammad (PBUH) settle the argument because they  all trusted him.[21] Also, his honesty during trade impressed Khadija, a wealthy businesswoman in Makkah, so much that she chose him as her representative in a trade expedition and later proposed to him for marriage.

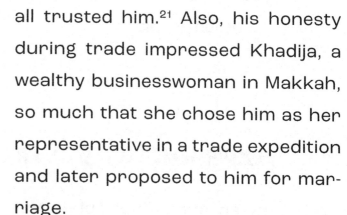

POSITIVE LESSON I CAN LEARN FROM OUR PROPHET (PBUH)

You can practice honesty by always telling the truth. You can be honest with your friends, always telling them the truth about how you feel, and with your family by giving your sincere opinion on something. Being honest keeps us closer to Allah and earns us the respect and trust of people.

HUMBLE

To be humble means that you don't consider yourself better than other people.

EXPERIENCE LIVED BY PROPHET MOHAMMAD (PBUH)

Allah sent an angel to Prophet Mohammad (PBUH) to give him a choice between being a servant-prophet or a king-prophet. He (PBUH) humbled himself upon the angel Gabriel's advice and chose to be a servant-prophet.[22] As a result, he (PBUH) lived his entire life as a servant.

He would mend his own shoes, repair his torn clothes, and milk his sheep. He would do all kinds of work, including digging into the ground during wars, carrying bricks and dirt for construction, cleaning, and collecting firewood. He would never recline while eating.[23]

POSITIVE LESSON I CAN LEARN FROM OUR PROPHET (PBUH)

Avoiding bragging and not showing off God's blessings means you are being humble. Giving credit where credit is due and congratulating your friend for a job well done is a sign of humility. Staying humble helps you become more responsible and helps you avoid becoming arrogant (thinking highly of yourself). It allows you to extend more compassion and empathy to others.

15

JUST

Being just is the quality of being fair and right when dealing with people.

EXPERIENCE LIVED BY PROPHET MOHAMMAD (PBUH)

Prophet Mohammad (PBUH) was a fair man. He would always make decisions based on truth and never on his desires or anyone else's requests. Once, a noble lady was brought to him who had been caught stealing. Since the lady had a high social status, people requested Prophet Mohammad

(PBUH) to be lenient with her. But the Prophet (PBUH) said he would treat her the same as any other person. He even said that if his daughter had stolen, he would punish her the same because that is fair.[24]

POSITIVE LESSON I CAN LEARN FROM OUR PROPHET (PBUH)

Treating everyone equally means being fair and just. If two friends at school ask you to judge a situation, or to give your opinion, you should be equitable and honest when giving your answer. To be just with everyone means you should be sincere with your judgment. Being fair will earn you people's respect and encourage others to do the same.

16

KEEP PROMISES

Keeping a promise is to do what we have promised we would do.

EXPERIENCE LIVED BY PROPHET MOHAMMAD (PBUH)

Prophet Mohammad (PBUH) kept his promises at all costs. Once, at a time of battle, a companion came to him and said that Quraish freed him on the condition that he wouldn't fight against them. He ordered him to keep his promise and return to Makkah, even though the Muslim army was small.[25] He had promised Quraish that if any Muslim came to Madinah after running away from Makkah, he would send them back. He kept his promise and sent a runaway companion back, even though it hurt him so much.[26]

I PROMISE!

POSITIVE LESSON I CAN LEARN FROM OUR PROPHET (PBUH)

Allah never breaks His promise and loves those who keep their promises. Keeping a promise that you made to a friend will increase people's trust in you, just as Prophet Mohammad's enemies trusted him (PBUH). Keeping a promise is the foundation for trust and respect. It leads to being reliable and having personal integrity. When you do what you say, and say what you do, you are setting a good example and becoming dependable.

KIND

Being kind is to be generous and helpful, and to think about other people's feelings.

EXPERIENCE LIVED BY PROPHET MOHAMMAD (PBUH)

Prophet Mohammad (PBUH) said, "Allah is kind and likes kindness in all things."[27] Hence, he was kind to everyone, including his family, relatives, children, the elderly, orphans, and even enemies. He never hit or raised his voice to children, women, or his servants. Instead, he always talked

to them gently. He would help his servants, hug and kiss children, and play with his family. He was also kind to animals. He prohibited us from hurting animals for sport[28] and advised us to be kind to them when slaughtering them.[29]

POSITIVE LESSON I CAN LEARN FROM OUR PROPHET (PBUH)

We should be kind to everyone, just like Prophet Mohammad (PBUH) was. If your friend or sibling gets hurt, don't hesitate to comfort him. Genuinely caring for others will make your heart happy. Being gentle and kind will help you nurture healthy relationships with others. You should also be kind to animals and never hurt them.

HAVE A SENSE OF HUMOR

Having a sense of humor is the quality of being funny and the ability to find things funny.

EXPERIENCE LIVED BY PROPHET MOHAMMAD (PBUH)

Prophet Mohammad (PBUH) was a light-hearted man. He was always seen smiling[30] and loved to keep the atmosphere happy using humor. He even said that smiling at your brother is a form of charity.[31] Once, a man came to him and asked for something to use for transporting goods. Prophet Mohammad (PBUH) said he would give him a baby camel (as a joke). The man was confused and said that no one could use a baby camel for transporting goods. Prophet Mohammad (PBUH) replied, "Every camel is always a baby of another camel."[32]

POSITIVE LESSON I CAN LEARN FROM OUR PROPHET (PBUH)

We should always try to find humor in simple things. Having a sense of humor helps keep the atmosphere light, make people smile, lift their mood, and strengthen the bonds between people. Having the ability to let go and not take everything so seriously is also having a sense of humor. So, if someone tries to make fun of you, laugh with them. Being good-humoured will also make your company more enjoyable to others.

MERCIFUL

Merciful means being willing to be kind and forgive people.

EXPERIENCE LIVED BY PROPHET MOHAMMAD (PBUH)

Allah says in the Quran, "And We have not sent you, [O Mohammad], except as a mercy to the worlds."[33] He was merciful to everyone, even his opponents. Once, a man asked him, "You kiss your children. I have ten children, and I have never kissed them." Prophet Mohammad (PBUH) replied, "Whoever does not show mercy will not receive mercy."[34] He was so merciful that he would let children play on his back even while he was praying. He would make his prostration long enough for them to finish playing.[35] He would even treat the captives of wars with great mercy.

POSITIVE LESSON I CAN LEARN FROM OUR PROPHET (PBUH)

Like our Prophet (PBUH) did, we should start by displaying mercy at home. If your parents or sibling are sick, you should take care of them. If your friend hurt you, you can show mercy by giving him or her a second chance. Being kind to those who offend you is to be merciful. Showing compassion to others, especially when we have been treated unfairly, will earn us Allah's mercy, both in this world and in the hereafter. Being merciful also helps strengthen our relationships with others.

MODEST

Being modest is the quality of not showing off your abilities, achievements, or attributes.

EXPERIENCE LIVED BY PROPHET MOHAMMAD (PBUH)

Prophet Mohammad (PBUH) was a modest man. He was highly successful in his mission of spreading Islam, but he never took pride in his success and always thanked and praised Allah for His help. He did not like people praising him or giving him special treatment because he was a prophet or a leader.[36] During different undertakings, his modesty did not allow him to sit and relax like a king while his companions worked hard. Instead, he participated and worked like everyone else.

POSITIVE LESSON I CAN LEARN FROM OUR PROPHET (PBUH)

Being modest is a positive attribute that every Muslim should have. You can show modesty by not bragging that you got a good grade at school. Accepting criticism and admitting you can be wrong from time to time is also an example of modesty. It's better not to show off our abilities, achievement, or attributes. It will help create a healthy atmosphere and strengthen our relationships with others.

OPTIMISTIC

Being optimistic is being able to see the positive in every situation.

EXPERIENCE LIVED BY PROPHET MOHAMMAD (PBUH)

Prophet Mohammad (PBUH) was an incredibly optimistic man. He always saw good, even in the worst of situations. When he went to Ta'if to teach people about Islam, their leaders rejected him and sent boys to mock him and throw rocks at him. He was hurt and sad. He was so optimistic that he had the firm conviction that even the children of such corrupt people would accept Islam one day and that they would do good deeds.[37] His optimism made him determined in his mission, inspired everyone and, ultimately, he succeeded in his mission.

POSITIVE LESSON I CAN LEARN FROM OUR PROPHET (PBUH)

We should always be optimistic, have a positive mindset, and hope for the best from Allah. If you feel like you are going through a difficult situation, try to focus on the positive. It doesn't mean that you should avoid or ignore the negative; rather, it involves making the most of a potentially bad situation. Being optimistic will help you accept that things don't always turn out how you want them to, and it will help you build resilience. Focusing on the good in every situation helps develop gratitude. It will also strengthen our trust in Allah and save us from unnecessary worries.

22

PATIENT

Being patient is the ability to wait, continue doing something despite difficulties, or endure without complaining.

EXPERIENCE LIVED BY PROPHET MOHAMMAD (PBUH)

Prophet Mohammad (PBUH) faced many difficulties and worries in his life, but he showed us the best example of patience every time. Sometimes, he faced hunger, but he never showed impatience. He was insulted when he preached Islam, but he patiently kept preaching. He lost his parents at an early age, and then his wife, Khadija, yet he always stayed patient and never complained. When his son, Ibrahim, died, Prophet Mohammad (PBUH) was distraught, but he said that, even though the heart is sad and the eyes are teary, we won't say anything that displeases Allah.[38] He never complained about anything and always thanked Allah for his blessings.

POSITIVE LESSON I CAN LEARN FROM OUR PROPHET (PBUH)

You can also be patient and follow the example of our Prophet (PUBH). Waiting in line for your turn without getting upset, or waiting for your parents or someone else to speak when you have something to say are simple examples of showing patience. Being patient will make you stronger. It will help you avoid being angry or worried when you must wait a long time for something, or when facing difficulties completing a task or project. Practicing your patience will build your confidence and decisiveness.

23

PEACE-LOVING

Being a peace-loving person refers to peace and trying to live and act in a way that will bring peace without violence.

EXPERIENCE LIVED BY PROPHET MOHAMMAD (PBUH)

Prophet Mohammad (PBUH) was a peace-loving man. He always tried to avoid fights and arguments by being forgiving and gentle with everyone. He ordered his companions to remain calm and peaceful in every situation, too. When Quraish presented the

treaty of Hudaibiya for him to sign, he happily agreed, even though the treaty contained many unfair points to the Muslims. He signed the treaty only to maintain peace between the Muslims and the disbelievers and avoid bloodshed.[39]

POSITIVE LESSON I CAN LEARN FROM OUR PROPHET (PBUH)

You can become a peace-loving person starting at home or school. Communicating your feelings instead of fighting with your friend or sibling, and being the first to calm a situation, means you are seeking peace. Maintaining peace and being opposed to violence will help you live a calm and happy life.

24
PERSEVERANT

To be perseverant means to have the ability to keep doing something despite difficulties.

EXPERIENCE LIVED BY PROPHET MOHAMMAD (PBUH)

The people of Quraish strongly opposed Prophet Mohammad (PBUH) and did everything to stop him from spreading the message of Allah. They abused him physically and verbally. They called him mad, a magician, and poet, and they accused him of defaming his forefathers. They boycotted him and his followers for three years, which caused him severe poverty. They forced him to emigrate to Madinah. They even tried to kill him. Despite all this, Prophet Mohammad (PBUH) continued to spread Islam without giving up for even a moment.[40]

POSITIVE LESSON I CAN LEARN FROM OUR PROPHET (PBUH)

Perseverance helps you achieve success. When facing difficulties during homework, or when preparing for an exam, you can persevere by staying focused, continuing to work hard, and not becoming discouraged. If you participate in a sports competition and keep training day after day, despite how difficult it is to do so, you are being perseverant. You can accomplish anything by persevering, just like Prophet Mohammad (PBUH) did.

RESPONSIBLE

Being responsible means honoring our commitments and accepting the consequences of our actions.

EXPERIENCE LIVED BY PROPHET MOHAMMAD (PBUH)

Prophet Mohammad (PBUH) was profoundly serious about his responsibilities. He was responsible for preaching Islam to everyone and took it seriously. He said that every one of us is responsible for whatever is in our keeping (family, livestock, material goods).[41] He also said that the best charity starts with caring for those

whom we are responsible for.[42] He used to visit each of his wives daily to ensure they were doing okay.[43] As a leader, he accepted his followers' responsibility regarding their religious and worldly affairs. He even considered himself responsible for the family of those who died poor.[44]

POSITIVE LESSON I CAN LEARN FROM OUR PROPHET (PBUH)

Being responsible means that you are doing what you are supposed to do. For example, you are responsible for getting ready on time for school in the morning or helping with certain household chores. Having responsibilities teaches you time management, self-discipline, and empathy. It will help you succeed and develop positive relationships.

26
SELF-SACRIFICING

A self-sacrificing person gives up what he wants so that others can have what they want.

EXPERIENCE LIVED BY PROPHET MOHAMMAD (PBUH)

Prophet Mohammad (PBUH) was a selfless man. His life revolved around worshipping Allah and serving his followers. He would sacrifice his own needs to make others happy. He made great sacrifices to teach Islam. His people abandoned him and boycotted him. He left Makkah and emigrated to Madinah to guide others to Islam. He also sacrificed great wealth and power offered by Quraish so he could preach Islam. He said he would teach Islam until death, even if they offered him the sun and the moon.[45]

POSITIVE LESSON I CAN LEARN FROM OUR PROPHET (PBUH)

Self-sacrificing is one of the most attractive qualities of our Prophet (PBUH). You can follow his steps by paying attention and seeing how you can help those in need. For example, giving away one of your favorite toys or your pocket money to someone in need instead of buying yourself some treats is self-sacrificing.

LIVE IN SIMPLICITY

Living in simplicity means being grateful for the little things in life and not always asking for more.

BE GRATEFUL, ENJOY THE LITTLE THINGS

EXPERIENCE LIVED BY PROPHET MOHAMMAD (PBUH)

Prophet Mohammad (PBUH) lived a simple life. He ate simple food, like barley bread,[46] wore simple clothes, and slept on a simple bed made of palm fibers. His house was so plain and simple that Umar (RA) cried when he saw it and said that the kings of Rome and Persia lived luxurious lives. Umar (RA) said that Prophet Mohammad (PBUH) was better than them, so he should have a better home. But Prophet Mohammad (PBUH) said he had chosen this over this Dunya.[47] He called himself a traveler in this world, so he had no interest in its luxuries.[48]

POSITIVE LESSON I CAN LEARN FROM OUR PROPHET (PBUH)

Living a simple life, like our Prophet (PBUH), helps make us less attached to material things. You don't need to buy everything that your friends bought. You don't need to buy more clothes or shoes if you already have enough. Appreciating what you have and not always asking for more will make your heart feel less worried, increase your happiness, and make you more grateful.

28

TRUTHFUL

Being truthful means being honest by always telling the truth.

EXPERIENCE LIVED BY PROPHET MOHAMMAD (PBUH)

Prophet Mohammad (PBUH) would never lie, even while joking. Quraish used to call him As-Saadiq, which means "the truthful," even before his prophethood. When Allah ordered him to teach Islam publicly, he gathered all the people of Quraish and asked them, "Would you believe me if I said that a caravan is going to attack you?" They all said they had never heard Mohammad (PBUH) lie, so they trusted him completely.[49] They knew he (PBUH) was speaking the truth about Islam, but they rejected it for political reasons.[50]

POSITIVE LESSON I CAN LEARN FROM OUR PROPHET (PBUH)

Allah forbids us from lying. Telling a lie, being dishonest, or cheating can make you feel guilty and fearful. Always tell the truth, no matter what, have positive intentions, make your actions match your words, and be sincere about your reactions. Being truthful help us gain Allah's love and people's trust and respect.

VALUE CLEANLINESS

To value cleanliness is to take good care of your hygiene.

EXPERIENCE LIVED BY PROPHET MOHAMMAD (PBUH)

Prophet Mohammad (PBUH) had an exceptionally clean and tidy life. He said, "Cleanliness is half of faith." He would oil and comb his hair and use perfume so he always smelled pleasant.[51] He would always wash himself to avoid germs and remain in the state of wudhu. He never blew or breathed inside a cup while drinking because that would add germs to the cup.[52] He would use Siwak to clean his teeth before every prayer. He would trim his nails, remove unwanted body hair, and trim down his mustache[53] every week because these things can hide many germs.

POSITIVE LESSON I CAN LEARN FROM OUR PROPHET (PBUH)

Taking care of your personal hygiene helps you stay healthy. For example, when you shower regularly, wash your hands when you return from school and before you eat, and brush your teeth throughout the day, especially before going to sleep, you are taking care of your hygiene. Being clean and keeping your environment clean by avoiding clutter will make you feel good. Others will also appreciate being around you, just like everyone loved to sit next to our Prophet (PBUH).

30
WELL-MANNERED

Being well-mannered means behaving pleasantly and politely.

EXPERIENCE LIVED BY PROPHET MOHAMMAD (PBUH)

Prophet Mohammad (PBUH) was a well-mannered man. He would always greet everyone. He would ask people about their well-being and of their loved ones. He would speak softly and gently. He never raised his voice or used bad words, even when someone insulted him. He would greet his guests graciously. He would let others speak and would listen to them attentively. Once, a young man started talking as part of a group conversation; Prophet Mohammad (PBUH) stopped him and said, "the eldest will speak first."[54]

POSITIVE LESSON I CAN LEARN FROM OUR PROPHET (PBUH)

Being well-mannered will make being in your company pleasant, just like everyone appreciated our Prophet (PBUH). For example, when you have family members over, try to enjoy their presence and avoid using electronics or playing video games. Instead, welcome them, be present, talk, play with them, and take the time to say goodbye when they leave. Being well-mannered will help spread love around you and help you become a better person.

We sincerely hope that you enjoyed this book.

If you believe we can further enhance our content,
please don't hesitate to contact us at :

INFO@GOODHEARTEDBOOKS.COM

Otherwise, feel free to rate and share your review.

Thank you!

REFERENCES

[1] Sahih al-Bukhari 1742 (Book 25, Hadith 220)
[2] Sunan Ibn Majah 425 (Book 1, Hadith 159)
[3] Sahih al-Bukhari 6012 (Book 78, Hadith 43)
[4] Sahih al-Bukhari 2910 (Book 56, Hadith 123)
[5] Sahih al-Bukhari 3149 (Book 57, Hadith 57)
[6] Sahih al-Bukhari 3922 (Book 63, Hadith 147)
[7] Sunan an-Nasa'i 825 (Book 10, Hadith 49)
[8] Sahih al-Bukhari 6125 (Book 78, Hadith 152)
[9] Sunan Ibn Majah 2248 (Book 12, Hadith 112)
[10] Masnad Ahmed 4568 (Book 75, Hadith 4568)
[11] Sahih Bukhari 603 (Book 10, Hadith 1)
[12] al-Sunan al-Kubrá 18275
[13] Sahih Bukhari 1277 (Book 23, Hadith 38)
[14] Sahih Muslim 2312a (Book 43, Hadith 78)
[15] Mishkat al-Masabih 146 (Book 1, Hadith 139)
[16] Sahih al-Bukhari 6307 (Book 80, Hadith 4)
[17] Jami' at-Tirmidhi 3640 (Book 49, Hadith 36)
[18] s-Sunan anl-Kubrâ (12477) and Ibn Katheer ibn al-Bidâya wan-Nihâya (3/218-219)
[19] How the Prophet Muhammad (PBUH) Rose above Enmity and Insult (Yaqeen institute)
[20] Zarqani vol.4 pg. 306
[21] Ar-Raheeq Al-Makhtum
[22] Related by al-Baghawee in Sharhus-Sunnah (no. 4683)
[23] Sunan Abi Dawud 3769 (Book 28, Hadith 34)
[24] Sahih al-Bukhari 3475 (Book 60, Hadith 142)
[25] Sahih Muslim 1787 (Book 32, Hadith 121)
[26] al-Jāmi' fī al-Sīra al-Nabawiyya. 6 vols.
[27] Sunan Ibn Majah 3689 (Book 33, Hadith 33)
[28] Sahih al-Bukhari 5479 (Book 72, Hadith 5)
[29] Riyad as-Salihin 639
[30] Jami' at-Tirmidhi 3641 (Book 49, Hadith 37)
[31] Jami' at-Tirmidhi 1956 (Book 27, Hadith 62)
[32] Sunan Abi Dawud 4998 (Book 43, Hadith 226)
[33] Quran, al-Anbiya' 21:107
[34] Sahih Muslim 2318a (Book 43, Hadith 86)
[35] Sunan an-Nasa'i 1141 (Book 12, Hadith 113)
[36] Sahih al-Bukhari 3445 (Book 60, Hadith 115)
[37] Ar-Raheeq Al-Makhtum
[38] Sahih al-Bukhari 1303 (Book 23, Hadith 61)
[39] Sahih Bukhari 2698, 2700 (Book 53, Hadith 8, 10)
[40] Ar-Raheeq Al-Makhtum
[41] Sahih al-Bukhari 2554 (Book 49, Hadith 37)
[42] Sunan an-Nasa'i 2544 (Book 23, Hadith 110)
[43] Sahih al-Bukhari 284 (Book 5, Hadith 36)
[44] Jami' at-Tirmidhi 2090 (Book 29, Hadith 1)
[45] Ar-Raheeq Al-Makhtum
[46] Jami' at-Tirmidhi 2360 (Book 36, Hadith 57)
[47] Sahih Muslim 1479e (Book 18, Hadith 44)
[48] Sahih al-Bukhari 6416 (Book 81, Hadith 5)
[49] Ar-Raheeq Al-Makhtum
[50] Ar-Raheeq Al-Makhtum
[51] Jami' at-Tirmidhi 2789 (Book 43, Hadith 62)
[52] Mishkat al-Masabih 4279 (Book 21, Hadith 115)
[53] Al-Adab Al-Mufrad Book 53: Circumcision (Book 1, Hadith 14)
[54] Sahih al-Bukhari 7192 (Book 93, Hadith 54)

Made in the USA
Las Vegas, NV
11 March 2024